If I really wanted to

Be Happy

I would . . .

RACINE, WI

If I Really Wanted to Be Happy, I Would . . .
ISBN: 978-1-970103-96-0 - *Paperback*
ISBN: 978-1-970103-97-7 - *Hardcover*
ISBN: 978-1-970103-49-6 - *Ebook*
Copyright © 2022 by Honor Books
Racine, WI

INTRODUCTION

Momentary happiness is fleeting and temporary; but true happiness, once discovered, invested in, and cherished grips the heart and inspires the life of the finder.

The simple insights contained in this small book cannot guarantee momentary happiness— nothing can! That's what they can't do. What they can do is far more exciting. The suggestions offered in these few short pages can help you enter into a lifestyle of happiness that is perpetually rewarding. They can help you rightly align yourself in regard to relationships and personal talents and abilities. They can even draw you closer to the Creator and His purpose for your life.

GOD BLESS YOU IN YOUR QUEST!

IF I REALLY WANTED TO
BE HAPPY, I WOULD . . .

LAUGH MORE -
ESPECIALLY AT
MYSELF

DO SOMETHING FOR YOUR HEALTH TODAY—LAUGH!

Laughter promotes good health, both in body and spirit. It not only brightens your mood but also eases tension. A good dose of laughter has been shown to improve blood circulation, stimulate digestion, lower blood pressure, and prompt the brain to release pain-reducing endorphins.

Laughter is also an expression of faith in God—it is the best response you can make to your own human frailties as you strive to live a happy life.

A cheerful heart is a good medicine.

PROVERBS 17:22 NRSV

IF I REALLY WANTED TO BE HAPPY, I WOULD . . .

FEED MY SOUL WITH A DOSE OF CREATION'S BEAUTY

IF YOU ARE TO FIND HAPPINESS, YOU MUST OPEN YOUR EYES TO SEE IT.

A woman on her way to work one chilly, overcast winter morning, was startled to see a path of pansies in bloom—their glorious purple and yellow hues were a stark contrast to the cloudy skies. Her mood instantly brightened. Those delicate flowers reminded her that beauty could be found on even the gloomiest of days and in the darkest of times, emotionally and spiritually.

When you take your eyes off your problems—even for a moment—you often find that God has placed something glorious in your path to cheer you on your way.

Beauty is a gift of God.

ARISTOTLE

TREAT MY BODY RIGHT

AS THE BODY GAINS STRENGTH, SO DOES THE INNER SELF.

Busy schedules sometimes mean that attention to exercise and good nutrition falls through the cracks. We all have these lapses, but the wise man or woman understands that neglecting the proper care of our bodies can be a serious obstacle to happiness.

Both exercise and nutrition are inextricably related to an internal sense of balance and emotional well being. Both are vital to energy levels, strength, and basic good health. Most importantly, both are directly related to a strong inner core of contentment, which can be your only link to happiness when the firestorms of life come your way.

Look to your health; and if you have it, praise God, and value it next to a good conscience; for health is the second blessing that we mortals are capable of; a blessing that money cannot buy.

IZAAK WALTON

IF I REALLY WANTED TO
BE HAPPY, I WOULD . . .

INVESTING MY RESOURCES IN THINGS OF LASTING VALUE

THE BEST INVESTMENT PORTFOLIO IS ONE LABELED "LOVE."

It's a wise man or woman who stops along the way to ask, "What resources do I have and how am I investing them?" Resources consist of more than finances; they also include time, love, energy, and all that God has given to you.

Take time out on a regular basis to give yourself a reality check. Are you responding to those things that seem urgent and neglecting those things that are most important? Take account of your investments today.

For where your treasure is, there your heart will be also.

MATTHEW 6:21 NIV

IF I REALLY WANTED TO
BE HAPPY, I WOULD . . .

GIVE MYSELF A BREAK

TO FORGIVE YOURSELF IS THE GREATEST GIFT OF ALL!

When faced with a challenge, it is always wise to ask for God's help, prepare to the best of your ability, give your most worthy effort . . . and then cut yourself a break! Nobody gets everything right every time; perfection belongs to God alone.

As difficult as it may be to accept, we all fail sometimes, even when we try hard to do well. The good news is that most people learn more from their failures than from their successes, and failures can create greater empathy and sensitivity for others. When you fail to forgive yourself for errors of human frailty, you disregard God's instruction to love yourself "just as you are" and frustrate your own path to happiness.

To err is human, to forgive, divine.

ALEXANDER POPE

IF I REALLY WANTED TO
BE HAPPY, I WOULD . . .

PLANT SOMETHING AND WATCH IT GROW

PLANT ... AND GROW RICH IN HAPPINESS.

Remember the simple assignment we were all given in elementary school—plant seeds in a cup of dirt and watch them grow? Didn't it seem unbelievable that a tiny seed could become a beautiful flower or tasty vegetable? What delight we took in watering the soil, putting the small pot in the sun, and watching the first green shoots emerge. It was a moment of life—a reminder of the mystery of growth, multiplication, and beauty that every living thing embodies.

That moment of pure happiness is easy to recapture. Find a small pot, fill it with soil, and plant your seeds. Then sit back and rediscover the wonder of it all.

Like the number of apples contained in an apple seed, each opportunity we seize holds an untold number of possibilities.

UNKNOWN

IF I REALLY WANTED TO
BE HAPPY, I WOULD . . .

BEGIN AND END EACH DAY WITH GENUINE THANKSGIVING TO GOD

COUNT YOUR BLESSINGS EVERY MORNING, AND THANK GOD FOR THEM ONE BY ONE!

Nothing invites happiness more than acknowledging the good things in your life and thanking God for them. Even when your circumstances are grim, you can always find something to be thankful for. Why is this important? Human nature causes us to focus on the negative, and the negative overwhelms our sense of inner contentment.

Rehearsing the positive aspects of your life will help you restore a delicate emotional balance and stabilize your inner compass. There is no better way to gain perspective and regain happiness.

Enter into his gates with thanksgiving, and into his courts with praise; be thankful unto him, and bless his name.

PSALM 100:4 KJV

IF I REALLY WANTED TO
BE HAPPY, I WOULD . . .

GIVE A CHILD A GENUINE COMPLIMENT

AS YOU SHAPE A CHILD, YOU SHAPE THE FUTURE AND RESHAPE YOURSELF.

Have you ever stopped to consider the maze of human relationships children must find their way through as they grow up? From each person and each relationship, they gather bits of information about their own strengths and weaknesses, as well as information about the best ways to communicate with and treat others.

Giving a child a genuine compliment teaches that child that he or she is intrinsically valuable, that he or she can trust those who tell the truth, that it is good to recognize strengths and abilities in others, and that compliments feel good! As they build up others, compliment-givers remind themselves of these same truths. See what you can do to help a child find the way.

If a child lives with praise, he learns to appreciate.

DOROTHY NOLTE

IF I REALLY WANTED TO BE HAPPY, I WOULD . . .

CONSISTENTLY CULTIVATE TIMES OF SOLITUDE

SOLITUDE STRENGTHENS AND
RENEWS THE SOUL AS MUCH AS
FOOD AND SLEEP STRENGTHEN
AND RENEW THE BODY.

As a vessel takes shape on a potter's wheel, the potter applies pressure to both the inside and the outside of the pot as it spins. Without the inside pressure, the pot would collapse inward. Without the outside pressure, the pot would not retain any shape.

Human beings also need strength from the inside to withstand the everyday pressures exerted from the outside. When we spend regular time in quiet solitude, listening to the heartbeat of God, we receive strength to withstand the pressures of life and respond to crises with faith and confidence.

Solitude is as needful to the imagination as
society is wholesome for the character.

JAMES RUSSELL LOWELL

IF I REALLY WANTED TO BE HAPPY, I WOULD . . .

SMILE AT STRANGERS

A SMILE IS A GIFT TO YOU AND TO OTHERS.

Few actions require so little and give back so much as a smile! Your smile to a stranger may be the only bright spot in that person's day, and there's a bonus in that smile for you as well. That's the great thing about smiles; they inspire happiness in both the receiver and the sender.

Add the "smile factor" to your daily routine for one week. Smile when you pass someone; smile at the folks in the elevator; smile at the motorist in the next car. Smile—smile—smile! You are sure to find your world less intimidating, your interactions with others more satisfying, and your personal happiness growing.

For I was hungry and you gave me something to eat, I was thirsty and you gave me something to drink, I was a stranger and you invited me in.

MATTHEW 25:35 NIV

IF I REALLY WANTED TO
BE HAPPY, I WOULD . . .

LOOK AT LIFE IN THE LIGHT OF GOD'S LOVE

WHEN WE TRULY STOP TO SEE
WHAT GOD HAS MADE FOR US TO
ENJOY, WE FIND HIS LOVE AT
EVERY TURN.

I n a meditation on the love of God written in the fourteenth century, Julian of Norwich wrote that God called her attention to a hazelnut she was holding in the palm of her hand. She marveled at it, so small, seemingly so insignificant, and yet suddenly valuable beyond measure because God had created it, had a purpose for it, and loved it. She concluded, "Everything owes its existence to the love of God."

Life is filled with these manifestations of God's infinite care. Open your eyes to see, and you too can experience the happiness of knowing that you are loved and valued by the Creator of the universe.

The voyage of discovery lies not in finding new landscapes, but in having new eyes.

MARCEL PROUST

IF I REALLY WANTED TO
BE HAPPY, I WOULD . . .

GIVE WHAT I DON'T NEED TO SOMEONE WHO HAS A NEED

BEING A PACK-RAT IS NOT A VIRTUE.

G o to your pantry and put your hand on a can of food that has been there for at least a year. Then go to any closet, drawer, or storage space in your home and pull out things you don't use. You're sure to find some items that you didn't even remember you owned.

Now consider this. Within a small radius of your home, no matter where you live, you will be able to find people who have little or nothing at all. Meeting someone else's need, even in a small way, is an incredibly gratifying experience and a major key to true happiness. Prepare a "gift from your surplus" for someone in need.

The measure of life is not its duration but its donation. How much will you be missed?

PETER MARSHALL

IF I REALLY WANTED TO BE HAPPY, I WOULD . . .

THANK SOMEONE!

DEVELOP AN ATTITUDE OF GRATITUDE.

No one is an island. From the day we are born until the day we die, we are dependent upon the help of others in countless ways. Who taught you to tie your shoes and button your buttons? Who stuck with you until you mastered long division or learned to read? Who encouraged you and helped you land your first job? Who taught you to love selflessly or encouraged you to use your talents to make a difference in the world?

As we grow older, our need for others becomes more acute. Our gratitude should grow in like measure. Today is a good day to call or write one of your "helpers" to say "Thanks!"

Give thanks to the Lord, for he is good.

PSALM 118:1 NIV

IF I REALLY WANTED TO
BE HAPPY, I WOULD . . .

REREAD A
FAVORITE BOOK

A PERSON NEVER OUTGROWS THE FUN OF VICARIOUS EXPERIENCES OR HAPPY ENDINGS.

A man was "caught" reading a children's novel from a series he had read when he was ten years old. He explained to his amused wife that as a child, he had been captivated by these stories about the old West, but that reading them again as an adult, he found himself enjoying the writing and imagery as much as the plot.

Books always have something new to offer. Reading a book you enjoyed as a child will help you recall happier times and rekindle a sense of pure adventure, discovery, and imagination. Find one of your old favorites and let it transport you back to a time of unfettered happiness and childlike wonder.

Books are the quietest and most constant of friends; they are the most accessible and wisest of counselors, and the most patient of teachers.

CHARLES W. ELIOT

IF I REALLY WANTED TO
BE HAPPY, I WOULD . . .

BE ALERT FOR THE "SMALL MIRACLES" THAT HAPPEN EVERY DAY

MIRACLES ARE YOURS FOR THE SEEING.

Miracles happen all around us every day. So often in fact that we routinely overlook them in the moment. It may be hours later that we realize God's miraculous protection surrounded us. It may be only upon quiet reflection that we recognize that being on time for an appointment despite numerous detours or finding a person in a crowd had a truly miraculous element to it.

Sometimes the miracles around you are as simple as a bud bursting into bloom or the hatching of birds' eggs outside your kitchen window. Taking time to see and appreciate the miraculous is guaranteed to bring a smile to your soul and happiness to your heart.

To me every hour of the light and dark is a miracle, every cubic inch of space is a miracle.

WALT WHITMAN

IF I REALLY WANTED TO BE HAPPY, I WOULD . . .

Rejoice with Those who Rejoice

TO MULTIPLY YOUR OWN JOY, ENJOY THE HAPPINESS OF OTHERS.

Many people find it easier to weep with those who weep than to rejoice with those who rejoice, because jealousy has a way of rearing its ugly head. Yet a sure way to greater and growing happiness is to celebrate the "good things" that come into the lives of others— allow their delight to become your delight.

If you truly are in relationship with other people, what they experience is, quite literally, a part of your experience. To count the good that happens to them as partly your own—without giving in to selfish impulses— will allow you to grow very rich, indeed, in joy, hope, and happiness.

I am glad and rejoice with all of you. So you too should he glad and rejoice with me.

PHILIPPIANS 2:17-18 NIV

IF I REALLY WANTED TO
BE HAPPY, I WOULD . . .

GIVE MYSELF A BOUQUET OF FRESH FLOWERS

GIVE YOURSELF A REMINDER OF THE GOODNESS AND BEAUTY GOD HAS CREATED.

Nothing brightens a room like a bouquet of fresh flowers! Flowers provide a splash of fresh and vibrant color to brighten the day and remind us of the beauty God has placed in the world. Flowers also speak of the fragility and delicacy of life and coax us to abandon our striving after the vain and the temporal. They echo to us the splendor of Eden and are a promise of the glory of Heaven.

As the English statesman William Wilberforce once said, "Lovely flowers are the smiles of God's goodness."

Flowers are the sweetest things God ever made
and forgot to put a soul into.

HENRY WARD BEECHER

If I really wanted to be happy, I would . . .

Go Fly a Kite!

TO FLY A KITE, YOU HAVE TO LOOK UP.

Charles Schulz, creator of the "Peanuts" comic strip, once noted that the reason he draws images of childhood is because we can all relate to moments when we were carefree and our biggest problem in life was keeping the kite out of the neighbor's tree.

On the next windy day, build or buy a kite, go to the nearest open field, let out the string, and let all your cares and worries go up, up, up, and away. Forget your adult responsibilities for a moment, and recapture the essence of unfettered happiness.

You will soon break the bow if you keep it always stretched.

PHAEDRUS

IF I REALLY WANTED TO BE HAPPY, I WOULD . . .

CHOOSE TO SEE THE BEST IN OTHERS

TELL SOMEONE TODAY WHAT YOU ADMIRE MOST ABOUT HIM OR HER.

Life is about choices, and one of the more important is how we view other people. We can choose to focus on an individual's good points or keep our eyes on those things that annoy us. We can choose to acknowledge and praise an individual's gifts, talents, contributions, and good work, or we can choose to be blind to the positive characteristics and see only their faults.

How you choose to see others, to a very great extent, becomes your opinion of your own self-worth. To see the good in others is to acknowledge that God is the giver of all good gifts and the author of love and acceptance.

Whatever is true, whatever is noble, whatever is right, whatever is pure, whatever is lovely, whatever is admirable— if anything is excellent or praiseworthy— think about such things.

PHILIPPIANS 4:8 NIV

IF I REALLY WANTED TO BE HAPPY, I WOULD . . .

EXERCISE, EXERCISE, EXERCISE

EXERCISE YOUR RIGHT TO BE HAPPY.

The human body is like the battery-toting bunny in television commercials—it will keep going and going if it is connected to the right energy source. Disregard the body's basic needs, however, and it will collapse right into the ground. One of the basic needs your body craves is regular exercise—heart-starting, blood-pumping, adrenaline-raising activity.

While exercise may seem inconvenient, boring, or tedious at times, its benefits are abundant, and keeping your body at its peak is sure to enhance your sense of general well being. What are you waiting for—get up and get going! One and two and one and two and . . .

Those who think they have not time for bodily exercise will sooner or later have to find time for illness.

EDWARD STANLEY

If I really wanted to be happy, I would . . .

Guard my Rest

A NAP IS A TERRIBLE THING TO WASTE!

The society we live in seems determined to pack as much as possible into every daywork, recreation, family time, good deeds— everything, it seems, but rest and relaxation. Our hectic lifestyles seem shortsighted in light of the fact that physicians say rest enhances the enjoyment and effectiveness of all our other efforts.

Rest, both physical and mental, will render you more alert, more productive, more efficient, and less irritable—in a word, happier! Use it as a baseline for all your other activities. Your body will thank you for it.

The end and the reward of toil is rest.

JAMES BEATTIE

IF I REALLY WANTED TO
BE HAPPY, I WOULD . . .

START THE DAY BY READING THE BIBLE

TAKE INTO YOUR HEART WHAT GIVES BOTH ABUNDANT LIFE NOW AND EVERLASTING LIFE IN THE FUTURE.

"Eat a good breakfast," that's what our moms used to say. Good nutrition in the morning imparts energy and strength for the entire day. That's the case with our spiritual energy and strength as well. Many believe that the Bible is the best source of spiritual nutrition, and at the very least, its pages are filled with sublime prose, extraordinary poetry, and practical wisdom.

As you begin, think about how each Scripture might apply specifically to you and the situations you are facing in the days ahead. The truths of the Bible are ageless and offer powerful guidance as you go through your days, weeks, and years. It truly is the fountain of eternal happiness.

Your word is a lamp to my feet and a light for my path.

PSALM 119:105 NIV

IF I REALLY WANTED TO BE HAPPY, I WOULD . . .

START SOMETHING AND FINISH IT

NOTHING FEELS BETTER THAN A JOB WELL DONE.

"There!" and "Whew!" are two of the most satisfying exclamations in the English language, especially when they punctuate the completion of a difficult task. Bringing a project or chore to completion evokes feelings of satisfaction, relief, and inner pride.

Someplace in your home or office is a task that has just been sitting there waiting for you to come along and lift your happiness quotient by completing it. Dive in and get it done! You'll be glad you did.

Success lies in the finishing, not the dreaming or the starting.

UNKNOWN

IF I REALLY WANTED TO BE HAPPY, I WOULD . . .

RECOGNIZE THAT "HAPPY" IS A CHOICE

TO EMBRACE HAPPINESS, YOU MUST FIRST LET GO OF MISERY.

Scarlett O'Hara, the foremost character in the classic Gone with the Wind, believed that only one thing would make her happy—becoming Mrs. Ashley Wilkes. When Ashley married another woman, Scarlett set out to make his life miserable, and in the process, she made her own life miserable. Rather than swallow her disappointment and make the best of things, she threw her happiness away with both hands.

Sure, happiness is an emotion, but it is also a choice. You can choose to be happy rather than sad, optimistic rather than pessimistic, or hopeful rather than doubtful. In that regard at least, no one can steal your happiness—it is yours to do with as you please.

Most folks are about as happy as they make up their minds to be.

ABRAHAM LINCOLN

IF I REALLY WANTED TO
BE HAPPY, I WOULD . . .

DO SOMETHING NICE FOR SOMEONE AND DO IT FIRST

GIVING FIRST TO OTHERS IS ULTIMATELY THE BEST GIFT YOU CAN GIVE TO YOURSELF.

Receiving is passive and an end in itself. But giving is active. It produces, generates, and creates. Those who give to others set into motion a cycle of blessing that often includes feelings of joy, happiness, satisfaction, fulfillment, and a deep, abiding sense of purpose. Nothing else in life produces so many benefits.

Giving first only serves to accentuate the experience. It is a genuine expression of love. Indeed, it is love's finest hour.

It is more blessed to give than to receive.

ACTS 20:35 TLB

SCHEDULE A "MENTAL HEALTH DAY" EACH QUARTER

TIME OFF TO GET IN TOUCH WITH YOURSELF AND GOD IS TIME WELL SPENT.

Try spending an entire day doing what is enjoyable, luxurious, special, and rewarding to your inner soul. It may be a day spent with dear friends or a day of walking in a beautiful setting, soaking in bubbles, indulging in an afternoon nap, or reading a good book by a roaring fire. Truly relax and enjoy your time apart from the busyness of life. Focus on things eternal, meaningful, and joyful.

These periodic personal retreats are guaranteed to make you feel refreshed and more balanced, with a fresh willingness to tackle the tasks at hand.

All work and no play makes Jack a dull boy and doesn't leave Jill with much of a shine either.

ROBERTA CULLEY

If I really wanted to be happy, I would . . .

Contact an Old Friend and Get Reacquainted

REACH OUT AND TOUCH THE
HAPPINESS OF YOUR YOUNGER
YEARS—CALL AN OLD FRIEND!

Friends from times past, especially from childhood, offer a unique perspective on our lives. They are associated with memories marked by greater innocence and purity. Lifelong friends are likely to be familiar with our family members, culture, church, school, or neighborhood. Getting back in touch can complete a circle, of sorts— providing a sense of wholeness, meaning, perspective, and personal warmth.

All friendships give us comfort and encouragement to face the future. Old friendships renewed also give the comfort and solace of times past.

The best mirror is an old friend.

GEORGE HERBERT

IF I REALLY WANTED TO
BE HAPPY, I WOULD . . .

PURSUE A LONG-NEGLECTED DREAM

TODAY IS THE DAY TO GO AFTER YOUR DREAM.

Anna longed to be an artist. Though she lacked paint, she used berry juice to satisfy her passion. However, after her marriage, she was forced to set her hobby aside. Life on the family farm, especially with a husband and children, kept her busy around the clock. She found a few minutes for embroidery in the evenings, but arthritis eventually made that pastime painful. Long past retirement age, she decided to return to her childhood joy. She picked up a paintbrush once again, and at age seventy-eight, began to sell her work.

Anna—whom we know as Grandma Moses — proved that it's never too late to find success and happiness doing something you love.

A longing fulfilled is sweet to the soul.

PROVERBS 13:19 NIV

IF I REALLY WANTED TO
BE HAPPY, I WOULD . . .

MAKE A NEW
FRIEND

YOU CAN ENLARGE YOUR HAPPINESS BY ENLARGING YOUR CIRCLE OF FRIENDS.

One of life's great blessings is to relax in the comfortable presence of old friends, where we are loved and accepted simply for who we are. We sometimes forget, however, that it was not always so. These dear and constant ones were once "new friends." God sent them across our paths so that we might expand our horizons and grow in new ways.

If you are wise, you will extend yourself to others and seek to forge new friendships. The older you are, the more difficult this might seem. But the rewards are great, and you are sure to find yourself refreshed and challenged.

Each friend represents a world in us, a world possibly not born until they arrive, and it is only by this meeting that a new world is born.

ANAIS NIN

IF I REALLY WANTED TO
BE HAPPY, I WOULD . . .

SCHEDULE A
"TEA TIME"
EVERY DAY

TIME OUT FOR TEA CAN MAKE YOU A HAPPY WORKER.

A corporation once instituted a "tea cart policy"—several persons pushed tea carts along the company hallways, pouring hot tea, and offering small sweet treats free-of-charge to employees at about three o'clock in the afternoon. The result was a dramatic increase in both productivity and quality of work during the remainder of the workday. Employees also registered a marked increase in their satisfaction with the firm and with their jobs.

Tea time provided four positive things for the employees: a restful break, a brief time to socialize with coworkers, a perceived "reward," and an energy boost. We all need these four things at least once a day! Suggest it to your boss, or prepare it for yourself.

Rest is not quitting the busy career; rest is the fitting of self to one's sphere.

JOHN SULLIVAN DWIGHT

IF I REALLY WANTED TO BE HAPPY, I WOULD . . .

BUY SOMETHING WHIMSICAL AT A GARAGE SALE

GIVE YOURSELF A GIFT TODAY
FOR NO REASON AT ALL!

The words of Jesus Christ recorded in the Bible admonish us to love others as we love ourselves. This runs contrary to the way many of us were taught, but ultimately it makes sense. You will be kinder to others when you have first been kind to yourself.

So don't be afraid to indulge in the occasional childlike pleasure, as long as it presents no danger for you or others. And these adventures in self-aggrandizement need not break the bank. A few cents for a garage sale treasure can leave you with a happy heart.

You must love others as much as yourself.

MARK 12:31 TLB

IF I REALLY WANTED TO
BE HAPPY, I WOULD . . .

MAKE THE CALL
I'VE BEEN PUTTING
OFF

DO THE RIGHT THING AND LET GOD DO THE REST.

There is no time like now for doing the thing you know is necessary but have been putting off. Procrastination undermines happiness, but being proactive can wash away frustration, anxiety, and uncertainty. Imagine how nice it will feel to have an unpleasant situation resolved or a damaged relationship on the road to healing.

If you're concerned about what another person may say in response to your apology, admission, or statement of truth, don't be. Regardless of the response, you will feel a powerful surge of happiness and relief because you have had the courage to do the right thing. Remember to speak with kindness.

By and by never comes.

ST. AUGUSTINE

IF I REALLY WANTED TO
BE HAPPY, I WOULD . . .

TAKE TIME TO THINK THROUGH IMPORTANT DECISIONS

Pause for happiness's sake.

We are wise to recognize that it takes only a few moments to weigh the potential consequences of a decision or to map out a plan that will bring increased effectiveness, efficiency, or quality. A pause to think can lead to a conclusion, "This is bad" or, "This is better." Both conclusions, either to avoid a negative path or to follow a more positive one, create the potential for greater success and less future suffering.

Don't let anyone place your happiness in jeopardy by rushing you to a decision before you're ready. Take your time and trust your instincts. You will have the answer precisely when you need it!

Swift decisions are not sure.

SOPHOCLES

IF I REALLY WANTED TO BE HAPPY, I WOULD . . .

PAY AS I GO

HAPPINESS CANNOT BE PURCHASED!

Reader's Digest once reprinted an article from Money magazine entitled, "Win Your War Against Debt." In the middle of the article, there was a two-page advertisement for a popular antidepressant! The irony of the placement of this ad may not have been intentional, but it conveyed a truth—debt can be depressing. Almost nothing zaps joy like a stack of unpaid bills marked "past due."

Some debt is unavoidable, but most indebtedness is self-inflicted. A "pay-as-you-go" policy is the best way to get out of debt and stay out of debt. And the happiness of a debt-free life cannot be calculated.

Let no debt remain outstanding, except the continuing debt to love one another.

ROMANS 13:8 NIV

Avoid Gossip

POSITIVE WORDS CREATE HAPPINESS AROUND YOU.

Good news travels fast and bad news travels faster. For some reason, people are more willing to pass along the negative things they hear than the positive. In so doing, they lose out on the positive return, for everything we say comes back to us eventually.

The road to true happiness is paved with compliments and praise. Such words bring a smile to both the speaker and the hearer and encourage the hearts of both. The positive things you say can also establish your reputation as a person of integrity, winning you the trust, admiration, and respect of others.

There is nothing that can't he made worse by telling.

TERRANCE

REINFORCE MY GOOD HABITS AND DUMP MY BAD HABITS

In building good habits, one builds a good life.

Good health, good relationships—the good life, in general, is never an accident. It is the clear and simple result of good living. When we establish habits that keep our lives on the right track, we can expect happiness to be a by-product.

Of course, it isn't possible to control every aspect of our lives. There will be times of sorrow and pain, even calamity, that will come to us simply because we live in an imperfect world. Nonetheless, if you establish good habits, you will be able to maximize and protect what God has given you. And remember, it only takes twenty-one days to establish a good habit.

Cultivate only the habits you are willing should master you.

Elbert Hubbard

IF I REALLY WANTED TO BE HAPPY, I WOULD . . .

BREAK INTO SONG

HAPPINESS IS BUT A FEW NOTES AWAY.

Deep at the core of every human being, God has placed the joy of song. This seems to be intended to counterbalance the more routine and troublesome aspects of life. Even if you can't carry a tune in a bucket as they say, releasing that urge to burst forth in song can leave you feeling renewed and invigorated.

In fact, singing has been known to be so energizing that individuals sometimes have trouble keeping their feet from tapping and their legs from springing forth in dance. Don't wait— sing for the joy of it, just because you can.

Sing to the Lord a new song; sing to the Lord, all the earth.

PSALM 96:1 NIV

IF I REALLY WANTED TO
BE HAPPY, I WOULD . . .

CHOOSE A CAREER BASED ON PERSONAL SATISFACTION RATHER THAN EARNING POTENTIAL

YOU MUST LEARN WHO YOU ARE BEFORE YOU CAN LEARN WHAT MAKES YOU HAPPY.

The ingredients necessary to produce genuine happiness vary from person to person, but one thing is true for all—material wealth or possessions never fully satisfy the inner longings of the human heart. Neither do they establish self-worth and fulfill our inner need for love.

Each person is a wonderful combination of distinct talents and passions, fitted together with a deep desire to express his or her God- given uniqueness. Take time to search out your own special giftedness and use it. When you do, happiness is sure to follow.

He is well paid that is well satisfied.

WILLIAM SHAKESPEARE

IF I REALLY WANTED TO
BE HAPPY, I WOULD . . .

SEE THE WORLD EVEN IF IT'S ONLY MY NEIGHBORHOOD

HAPPINESS IS DISCOVERING THE WORLD AROUND YOU.

Think for a moment about those places you'd most like to see and map a plan for going there. Another state? Another nation? Why live like a hamster in a wheel, running in the same rut every day to the same places at the same times? Take time out! Establish a timetable for embarking on your personal adventure. The truth is, that half the happiness is in the anticipation. So dream big and often!

And in the meantime, take time out to discover the treasures in your own back yard and neighborhood. There's an amazing world within a few miles waiting to be discovered and enjoyed.

Voyage, travel, and change of place impart vigor.

SENECA

IF I REALLY WANTED TO BE HAPPY, I WOULD . . .

BECOME A FEARLESS "DO-GOODER"

HAPPINESS COMES BACK TO YOU
WHEN YOU GIVE IT AWAY.

Organizations like Habitat for Humanity have found that if fifty people join together, they can build or refurbish a house for a needy family. And if building a house is not quite your "cup of tea," there are plenty of other possibilities that will allow you to invest your time, energies, and talents in a good cause without bearing the entire responsibility or expense.

Look for a project in your neighborhood or town, and if you can't find one that seems right for you, start your own and invite others to take part. There is nothing quite as gratifying as the selfless act of helping others—nothing that will remind you so boldly of all God's goodness in your own life.

A good man produces good deeds from a good heart.

LUKE 6:45 TLB

IF I REALLY WANTED TO
BE HAPPY, I WOULD . . .

TACKLE
DIFFICULT CHORES
FIRST

Don't Work Harder; Work Smarter!

Whatever you find most difficult to do—take it on first. It's best to tackle tougher tasks early in the day when energy and motivation are both at peak levels. This little trick will help you complete jobs more quickly and with fewer complications. Plus, getting the tough task out of the way gives satisfaction and momentum to the rest of the day.

You may be thinking that you would be happiest with no chores at all. Perhaps you're right, but that would not be the case with most human beings. Work and the satisfaction it brings seems to be a key ingredient in our human happiness quotient.

Far and away the best prize that life offers is the chance to work hard at work worth doing.

Theodore Roosevelt

IF I REALLY WANTED TO
BE HAPPY, I WOULD . . .

REWARD MYSELF
FOR WORTHY
GOALS OR DEEDS

IT TRULY IS GOOD TO DO GOOD.

Rewards motivate us to keep doing what we know to be good, right, and just. They help us overcome the inertia of laziness and apathy. For that reason, we can use personal rewards as a way to increase our capacity for doing the right things.

As the old song declares, "Accentuate the positive . . . eliminate the negative!" The more we reward the positive, the more we turn our attention and efforts, and the attention and efforts of others, away from those things that destroy or cause harm and toward those things that bring happiness and fulfillment.

The laborer is worthy of his reward.

1 TIMOTHY 5:18 KJV

IF I REALLY WANTED TO BE HAPPY, I WOULD . . .

GIVE AND RECEIVE MORE HUGS

HUMAN TOUCH CONNECTS US SPIRITUALLY AND PHYSICALLY TO OTHERS.

Hugs are powerful—they can take the hurt out of a child's scraped knee, heal a longstanding alienation, soothe a troubled soul, comfort the grieving heart, and put a smile on the face of almost any person who gives or receives one. Hugs are an expression of love without words. They speak for themselves, saying, "I care, I accept you, I value you, I've missed you, I like to be with you, I'm here for you."

Hugs are necessary for emotional growth— in fact, some researchers have concluded that children need as many hugs a day as they need glasses of milk. And marriage counselors often prescribe that spouses should hug at least twice a day. Don't forget to take your "hug for happiness" today!

Love gives us in a moment what we can hardly attain by effort after years of toil.

VON GOETHE

IF I REALLY WANTED TO
BE HAPPY, I WOULD . . .

PLAY A
CHILDREN'S GAME
WITH A CHILD

INNOCENT FUN IS THE BEST FUN OF ALL.

Children play spontaneously and freely for the sheer fun of it. Many adults think that such play is childish. The truth is, we could all use an occasional adventure in the innocence and unfettered delight of a child's world.

Find yourself a little person and ask if he or she has any "fun" games the two of you could play together. You might be surprised how much happiness such an activity can produce—after all, there's nothing to prove and plenty to gain. Even if you lose, you're sure to come away smiling.

We find delight in the beauty and happiness of children that makes the heart too big for the body.

RALPH WALDO EMERSON

IF I REALLY WANTED TO
BE HAPPY, I WOULD . . .

BE QUICK TO ASK FOR FORGIVENESS

THE BEST STATE TO LIVE IN IS THE STATE OF "FORGIVEN."

F orgiveness is a wonderful thing and yet, much too often we allow our stubbornness to keep us burdened down with guilt, struggling with broken relationships and feeling inadequate. The good news is that no one needs to live that way.

When we ask for forgiveness from God and those we have hurt or offended, we turn the tables on guilt and shame. A rush of joy, peace, and even elation soon follows. Why sit huddled in a dark corner of the doghouse when you can be running and playing in the sunshine of forgiveness? And remember, sometimes you need to forgive yourself.

Blessed are they whose transgressions are forgiven.

ROMANS 4:7 NIV

IF I REALLY WANTED TO BE HAPPY, I WOULD . . .

TAKE COOKIES TO A FRIEND OR NEIGHBOR

IF YOU WANT HAPPINESS, GIVE SOME AWAY.

Food has been an important means of expressing acceptance and hospitality in virtually every culture throughout recorded history. It is such a natural act that a young child is likely to offer a half-eaten cracker to a stranger.

There are undoubtedly many complex reasons why human beings feel this need to share; however, it is enough for us to know that such an exercise brings with it a strong sense of well-being. Somehow when you give an offering of happiness to someone else, it comes back to perch on your own windowsill!

The heart benevolent and kind the most resembles God.

ROBERT BUMS

SMILE THE MOMENT I WAKE UP IN THE MORNING

SMILING GETS YOUR FACE IN THE MOOD TO BE HAPPY.

Set a tone of happiness for the day by smiling as soon as you wake up each morning. Smile first at God, saying in your heart, Thank You for watching over me all night. Smile second at the remembrance of at least one good thing that happened the day before. Smile third at the thought of all the opportunities and blessings that await you during the day. Smile fourth at the thought that God will be present throughout the day to help you with every crisis, challenge, or obstacle. Smile fifth at the very fact that you are alive and smiling.

As you smile, ask for God's grace to give away your five smiles to others before retiring for the night.

The more you are thankful for what you have,
the more you have to be thankful for.

ZIG ZIGLAR

PAUSE BEFORE RESPONDING TO AN ANGRY OR CRITICAL REMARK

SELF-CONTROL IS THE GIFT OF PATIENCE.

N ever allow another person to control you. Demonstrate your self control to yourself and others by pausing for ten seconds before you answer an angry or critical remark.

When we respond too quickly, the tendency is to overreact and fan the flames of conflict. A timely pause not only gives you a chance to speak calmly, rationally, and thoughtfully, but it also provides an opportunity for the other person to reconsider his or her words. It's difficult to be happy when we let others engage us in conflict. But it feels down-right satisfying when you know you have handled a tricky situation with finesse.

A soft answer turneth away wrath.

PROVERBS 15:1 KJV

IF I REALLY WANTED TO BE HAPPY, I WOULD . . .

LEARN SOMETHING NEW EVERY DAY

DEVELOP A LEARNING YEARNING.

Graduation ceremonies are called "commencement exercises," because they mark the beginning rather than the end of our learning process. Formal education simply equips us with the skills we need to process information and expand our minds throughout our lifetimes. Learning never ends!

The more we learn, the more we want to learn! The person who makes it a habit to learn something new, awakens each day with a true zest for living—an expectancy and eagerness to discover even more about the world God has created and those He has placed in it.

Learning is discovering a new world, a new galaxy, a new species. It keeps you ageless.

UNKNOWN

IF I REALLY WANTED TO BE HAPPY, I WOULD . . .

FOCUS ON THE BEST IN MYSELF

BUILD THE GOOD THAT YOU ARE
INTO THE BEST YOU CAN BE.

Most people tend to focus on those aspects of their personality and appearance that they would most like to change. Admit it now! Don't you hear yourself saying something like, "If only my feet were smaller, my hair thicker, and my ears flatter." That kind of thinking only leads to dissatisfaction and low self-esteem.

The true seeker of happiness will find a way to focus on those things others admire and like most about him or her—and celebrate them! Focusing on your best characteristics can literally help you to see your life in a better light. After all, we are each God's unique creation.

Praise yourself daringly, something always sticks.

FRANCIS BACON

IF I REALLY WANTED TO BE HAPPY, I WOULD . . .

ERR ON THE SIDE OF GENEROSITY

GIVING IS A RICH WAY OF LIVING.

Truly happy people are routinely generous. Whether they have little or much, they have discovered the joy of sharing with others freely and abundantly. Such people are sometimes short on cash, but they are always rich in the things that money cannot buy.

Practice generosity in your own life. If you are already a generous person, press yourself to be generous until it hurts. You will soon notice that your attitudes about money and possessions are changing, your relationships are flourishing, and your outlook on life is bright.

A generous man will prosper; he who refreshes others will himself he refreshed.

PROVERBS 11:25 NIV

IF I REALLY WANTED TO
BE HAPPY, I WOULD . . .

REGARD AGE AS A GIFT

AGE IS A SACRED TRUST.

Getting older is a lot more than adding wrinkles, submitting to aches and pains, and watching your children leave home. Age is a record of your days. And it bears gifts— namely wisdom and confidence.

So continue to celebrate those birthdays. Think back over the challenges you have conquered in the past year. Remember the victories, and cherish new accomplishments. Catalog the insights you've recently acquired, and thank God once again for every day He has given you.

Life is most delightful when it is on the downward slope.

SENECA

IF I REALLY WANTED TO BE HAPPY, I WOULD . . .

USE THINGS AND LOVE PEOPLE

TRUE WEALTH AND TRUE HAPPINESS COME FROM LOVING RELATIONSHIPS.

We live in a consumer culture—one that values possessions and experiences more than people. And yet, somehow we know that these things can never give to the human heart what it desires most: loving relationships and a sense of self-worth.

To experience genuine happiness, it is necessary to strike a balance between the pursuit of things and a solid investment in the lives of others. The best of all plans is to use things for the purpose of expressing love to others.

LOVE SEEKS TO MAKE HAPPY RATHER THAN TO BE HAPPY.

IF I REALLY WANTED TO BE HAPPY, I WOULD . . .

CHASE A BUTTERFLY

HAPPINESS IS SOARING WITH THE WINGS YOU HAVE BEEN GIVEN.

Until the Wright brothers did what seemed impossible, man was unable to take to the skies. How far we have flown since then! And yet, no flying machine has ever matched the beauty of a butterfly, as it colors the air of a garden with its vibrantly designed wings.

The mystery and beauty of the butterfly lies beyond its ability to fly—in its miraculous transformation from a lowly caterpillar. Through its example, we discover that the grounded and limited can soar in unlimited flight, the bound and lifeless can be free and vibrant, the dull and colorless can become beautiful and inspiring. Chase a butterfly, and glimpse the power of the possible.

But those who hope in the Lord will renew their strength. They will soar on wings like eagles.

ISAIAH 40:31 NIV

IF I REALLY WANTED TO
BE HAPPY, I WOULD . . .

TREAT MYSELF TO A "CULTURAL" EXPERIENCE

Part of feeling happy is feeling connected.

A woman once took her young son to an art exhibit, unsure of exactly how he might respond to the imposing gallery, the crowd of adults, the silence of the great halls, and the pieces on display that defied comprehension. As they stood facing a modern painting, which may have been hung upside down for all the mother could tell, her son spoke up, "I like this one. It's how I feel sometimes."

Art, music, and dramatic performance speak to each of us—sometimes in unexpected ways but always in deep and wonderful ways. The artistic expressions of our culture send a message that we are not alone in our feelings or isolated in our experiences.

Every artist dips into his own soul, and paints his own nature into his pictures.

HENRY WARD BEECHER

IF I REALLY WANTED TO
BE HAPPY, I WOULD . . .

BEGIN EACH DAY
BY GIVING
THANKS

SAYING THANKS IS THE BEST WAY TO COUNT YOUR BLESSINGS.

We are accustomed to giving thanks at the dinner table, but have we considered the benefits of doing so at the beginning of each day? Such an exercise can serve to guide us toward attitudes of love, forgiveness, and mercy and remind us that we are, in fact, even now, surrounded by happiness.

Begin today by thanking God for the simple things in life that bring great joy. Thank Him for honest and useful work and the skill to perform it. Thank Him for the resources He has provided to meet your daily needs. Thank Him for the love of family and friends. And thank Him for the breath of life.

Be anxious for nothing, prayerful for everything, thankful for anything.

D. L. MOODY

IF I REALLY WANTED TO
BE HAPPY, I WOULD . . .

BE CAREFUL NOT TO BITE OFF MORE THAN I CAN CHEW

CANDLES AREN'T MEANT TO BE BURNED AT BOTH ENDS.

There is a point of diminishing return for all endeavors, where quantity conflicts with quality and pressure to perform conflicts with morale and good relationships. Over-commitment is a fast path to burnout. And no person can be truly happy if he or she is stressed to the max.

Most people feel that "no" is an unhappy word. But learning to say "no" can provide balance to your life and allow you the time you need to stop and smell the roses. It will also free up your schedule so that you can say "yes" to those things you really want and need to be involved in. Do what you can for yourself and others. Then leave the rest in the hands of God.

The wisdom of the prudent is to give thought to their ways.

PROVERBS 14:8 NIV

IF I REALLY WANTED TO
BE HAPPY, I WOULD . . .

TRUST IN THE GOODNESS OF OTHERS

WE ALL BENEFIT WHEN OTHERS ARE GIVEN THE BENEFIT OF THE DOUBT.

The owners of a Florida restaurant instituted a "no bill" policy. At the end of the meal, diners were given "offering" envelopes. Over time, the owners discovered that some enclosed the true value of the meal, some left nothing or less than the meal's value, and some gave more than their meal cost to prepare and serve.

This might seem naive, and of course, there were customers who took advantage of the opportunity to skip out and pay nothing. But overall, the trust the owners placed in their customers has been rewarded. And everyone feels good about it. There is a special joy in trusting people to do the right thing.

Trust men and they will he true to you; treat them greatly and they will show themselves great.

RALPH WALDO EMERSON

IF I REALLY WANTED TO BE HAPPY, I WOULD . . .

SAY "I LOVE YOU"

THE MOST IMPORTANT WORDS IN THE ENGLISH LANGUAGE ARE "I LOVE YOU."

The paper was poorly folded. The writing was smudged and crooked. The verse didn't rhyme, and the cutout of a heart made less than a perfect Valentine. But the message from the young girl to her mother was clear: "I love you."

Don't wait to express your love for others. No matter how you package it, this gift is certain to bring happiness to your life and the lives of others. And failing to do so, can bring you a heart full of regret when the opportunity is lost. It takes so little in the way of time, energy, and resources. Do it for yourself and someone you love today.

Speech both conceals and reveals the thought of men.

DIONYSIUS CATO

IF I REALLY WANTED TO
BE HAPPY, I WOULD . . .

LEARN TO
RECEIVE FROM
OTHERS

THOSE WHO RECEIVE WELL, GIVE A GIFT IN RETURN.

When you acknowledge a gift as an expression of love, you give a gift of "appreciation" and loving "recognition" in return. An enthusiastic and thankful receiver creates an atmosphere of celebration for everyone and allows the giver to experience a moment of true happiness.

Delight in every gift—whether small or large! Relish the party given in your honor—others will feel freer to enjoy themselves. Express appreciation when others come alongside to help—they will be more eager to help again. It's a great feeling to let someone else shine.

How grateful I am and how I praise the Lord
that you are helping me again.

PHILIPPIANS 4:10 TLB

IF I REALLY WANTED TO
BE HAPPY, I WOULD . . .

TRY A NEW FLAVOR OF ICE CREAM

SIMPLE PLEASURES CAN SATISFY COMPLEX NEEDS.

Life's simple pleasures are often life's greatest pleasures. A new flavor of ice cream, a walk in the rain, a single fresh flower, a warm slice of homemade bread, taking time to watch an entire sunset unfold—each can be a delight to the senses and bring about a greater sense of well-being.

Simple pleasures are those that don't need to be "saved for" or put off until vacation time. They are readily available to evoke the feelings of contentment and satisfaction that soothe frayed nerves. They give an extraordinary quality to otherwise "ordinary" days. And best of all, they nearly always can be shared.

Pleasure in moderation relaxes and tempers the spirit.

SENECA

IF I REALLY WANTED TO
BE HAPPY, I WOULD . . .

LET OTHERS KNOW WHEN I THINK GOOD THOUGHTS ABOUT THEM

MAKE SOMEBODY'S DAY BY BEING A BEARER OF GLAD TIDINGS!

There is no better day than today for you to express the good thoughts you have for others. Too often we wait for special occasions to tell others what they mean to us or that we are grateful for their presence in our lives. Whether it is to simply wish someone well, convey a sense of pride, or thank them for their kindness and support, your words cannot work for you if they are left unspoken.

When was the last time you told your spouse, your children, or one of your friends how much they mean to you? When you give someone else a reason to be happy, you will be happier too.

Words are the soul's ambassadors, who go abroad upon her errands to and fro.

JAMES HOWELL

IF I REALLY WANTED TO
BE HAPPY, I WOULD . . .

CHERISH EVERY SPECIAL OCCASION

SPECIAL OCCASIONS ARE THE TIES THAT BIND.

Rituals are important because they serve as markers for our lives and relationships. Many people think that rituals are always religious in nature, but birthday parties, anniversary celebrations, award ceremonies, family gatherings, vacations, holiday dinners, even the fishing trips we take with a son or daughter are cultural rituals that unite us and enhance our connectedness.

Embrace the cultural rituals in your life. Take pictures and remember together. Memorialize family stories: "Hey do you remember when Grandpa Brink did . . . ?" Cherishing special times will allow you to store up your happiness for the hard times that are sure to come to us all.

It is right to celebrate.

LUKE 15:32 TLB

PUT ASIDE
PREJUDICE AND
STEREOTYPES

PREJUDICE CANNOT COEXIST WITH
LOVE. ONE WILL ALWAYS PREVAIL
TO THE EXCLUSION OF THE OTHER.

P rejudice and stereotypes are both blinding and binding. They keep us from experiences that can help us grow and develop character. Prejudice is not limited to race—it can be directed toward gender, age, ethnic origin, economic status, and religion, to name just a few. One woman even admitted she was "prejudiced against those who are prejudiced."

On the flip side, putting aside prejudice can open wide the doors of friendship, wellbeing, and cultural appreciation. It can expand the boundaries of our minds and enhance our knowledge of the world around us. Breaking the bonds of prejudice is like bursting forth from a cocoon to fly free and happy in the sunshine.

You must look into people as well as at them.

LORD CHESTERFIELD

IF I REALLY WANTED TO BE HAPPY, I WOULD . . .

SING IN THE SHOWER

MAKING A JOYFUL NOISE CAN MAKE A JOYFUL HEART.

Luciano Pavarotti, Leontyne Price, Barbra Streisand, and others have become famous primarily because of their superb singing voices. They make it easy for us to close our eyes and be magically swept up in the emotions of happiness, love, and contentment.

Few are blessed with such talent, but we can all belt out a tune in the shower. For a few happy moments, we can become one of the world's great singers, flooding the air with our own interpretations of personal favorites. Singing strengthens the lungs, exercises the diaphragm, and brings light to the soul. Try it and see for yourself.

He who sings scares away his woes.

CERVANTES

IF I REALLY WANTED TO
BE HAPPY, I WOULD . . .

LISTEN TO THOSE WHO ARE WISE

THE WISE NEVER STOP SEEKING WISDOM.

Depth perception tells us how close or far away certain objects are. Those with impaired vision in one eye lack accurate depth perception and have a decreased ability to make contact with or avoid objects.

The principle that two eyes are better than one extends far beyond physical eyesight. Wise mentors give us depth perception in regard to situations and circumstances. They help us make contact with success and stay out of harm's way. And when you consider that the amount of happiness in our lives is to a certain extent dependent upon the choices we make, it seems right to seek the advice of wise and caring people.

Apply your heart to instruction and your ears to words of knowledge.

PROVERBS 23:12 NIV

IF I REALLY WANTED TO BE HAPPY, I WOULD . . .

TRY A NEW RECIPE

SOMETHING INSPIRATIONAL!

The amazing and mysterious aspects of food have been known and appreciated since the beginning of recorded history. In fact, the whole Garden of Eden episode boils down to Eve's desire to sample a new fruit and serve it to her husband. If you've experienced the delight and exhilaration of trying a new dish, then you probably understand what happened there in the Garden that fateful day.

Fortunately, all experiments in dining do not carry such daunting consequences. So when you need a "happiness kick," consider opening a recipe book and trying something daring and delicious. Today's cookbooks are simple enough for even the uninitiated to follow with ease. Bon Appetite!

The discovery of a new dish does more for human happiness than the discovery of a new star.

ANTHELME BRILLAT-SAVARIN

GIVE UP THE IDEA OF CHANGING OTHERS

THE ONLY ONE YOU CAN
EFFECTIVELY CHANGE IS YOURSELF.

One of the greatest and most liberating moments in life is the one when we realize we cannot change other people. No matter how much we love them or they love us— such change is entirely a function of personal will and God's grace.

Give love freely and unconditionally, accentuating the strengths and encouraging the good in those around you. Don't become an enabler of hurtful or damaging behavior, but also remember that each person is ultimately responsible for his or her personal choices. People do change—often profoundly and genuinely— but such change must come from within.

Consider how hard it is to change yourself and you'll understand what little chance you have of trying to change others.

JACOB M. BRAUDE

IF I REALLY WANTED TO BE HAPPY, I WOULD . . .

BE KIND TO STRANGER

THERE ARE NO STRANGERS, ONLY PEOPLE WHO DON'T KNOW EACH OTHER YET.

An old tombstone reads, "He never met a stranger." What volumes that brief message conveys about the man buried there! It is easy to imagine that he was quick to laugh and quick to empathize, to the point of shedding a tear. It is easy to imagine his small acts of kindness to those who never knew the source of their "pleasant surprise."

What a great epitaph! And what an avenue for inner happiness. Helping strangers is pure and unconditional. By its very nature, it has no strings attached. When you help a stranger, it serves as a gift of appreciation to God.

I was a stranger, and ye took me in.

MATTHEW 25:35 KJV

IF I REALLY WANTED TO BE HAPPY, I WOULD . . .

LEARN SOME GOOD JOKES

Laughter is the Sound of Happiness.

Humor and its side-effect, laughter, have been shown to improve both blood pressure and heart rate in seriously ill people. It is, in fact, so therapeutic that clowns are permanent employees in most major children's hospitals. A little humor can heal broken relationships, defuse angry situations, and provide a much- needed perspective.

Invest some humor in your life by searching out and learning good jokes. They should be easy to remember and pass your own humor test. Never choose a joke that denigrates others—that is simply not funny. Stick with good taste and leave 'em rollin'.

The most completely lost of all days is that one on which one has not laughed.

Chamfort

IF I REALLY WANTED TO
BE HAPPY, I WOULD . . .

RESPECT THE FEELINGS OF OTHERS

RESPECT, WHETHER GIVEN OR RECEIVED, IS ITS OWN REWARD.

Every person has a built-in need to be heard, understood, and respected. The key is to remember that respect is a sword that cuts two ways. What we need most comes to us as we give it away to others.

Learning to really listen and developing sensitivity for the needs of others is most often a matter of simple practice. When listening to others, learn to focus on them and give them your full attention. Resist the urge to interrupt or mentally construct your reply, and don't be tempted to judge or instruct. Listening validates the speaker and conveys respect and caring. In giving, you shall receive.

The first duty of love is to listen.

PAUL TILLICH

IF I REALLY WANTED TO
BE HAPPY, I WOULD . . .

ALWAYS KEEP CONFIDENCES

HAPPINESS IS KEEPING SAFE THAT WHICH HAS BEEN COMMITTED UNTO US.

Secrets can be wonderful and therapeutic. They can bring us great joy and emotional release. They can strengthen the bond between people and allow us to share in the happiness of others. Sharing of confidences can also mean that people trust you enough to make themselves vulnerable. When that happens, there is great virtue in keeping the confidence.

Protecting the secrets others confide in you is an expression of love. It is a guarding of relationship and a privileged responsibility. Its reward is a good night's sleep, strengthened character, and constant friendship.

A gossip betrays a confidence, but a trustworthy man keeps a secret.

PROVERBS 11:13 NIV

IF I REALLY WANTED TO BE HAPPY, I WOULD . . .

DEVELOP MY TALENTS

PRACTICE ALWAYS BRINGS US CLOSER TO OUR OWN PERFECTION.

Educational researchers have concluded that most people have between three and five major talents, each of which can be developed and applied in a way that will benefit others. Remember though, having talent is easy; developing that talent requires time, effort, and long-term commitment.

Discovering and developing your own specific talents can be one of the happiest and most satisfying journeys of your life. The more you do what you were created to do, the greater your sense of fulfillment, purpose, and inner satisfaction. Go ahead and mine your own gold!

A winner is someone who recognizes his talents, works his tail off to develop them, and uses them to achieve his goals.

LARRY BIRD

IF I REALLY WANTED TO
BE HAPPY, I WOULD . . .

REFLECT ON
GOD'S AWESOME
UNIVERSE

LOOK UP AND SEE WHAT GOD HAS DONE.

Childlike wonder is always in vogue. And wonder, we must, when we consider the vastness and splendor of the universe. The more we study its intricacies and delve into its mysteries, the more we are compelled to acknowledge that the "secret of life" and the "meaning of existence" cannot be reduced to an equation or formula. They are cradled lovingly in the hand of God.

So if it is happiness that you truly desire, wander outside some clear starlit night and take a few moments or hours to gaze up into the cosmos. Allow your troubles to melt away as they are juxtaposed against a blanket of twinkling miracles.

When I consider your heavens, the work of your fingers, the moon and the stars, which you have set in place, what is man that you are mindful of him, the son of man that you care for him?

PSALM 8:3-4 NIV

Always Tell the Truth, the whole Truth, and Nothing but the Truth

SEEK THE TRUTH. THEN SPEAK THE TRUTH.

Happy people know better than to compromise the integrity of their souls for the sake of the moment. They cling to truthfulness and carefully guard their hearts from deception. Why? Because they have learned that telling the truth makes it easier to sleep at night, inspires the loyalty of their friends, and earns them the respect of all.

Nonetheless, honesty, pure and undiluted, is rare in our society today. It has fallen prey to convenience and a misguided belief that lying to people will help them in the end. Sure, truth is often painful, but it can also be your best friend.

Half the truth is often a great lie.

BENJAMIN FRANKLIN

IF I REALLY WANTED TO
BE HAPPY, I WOULD . . .

APPRECIATE
WHAT I HAVE

HAPPINESS IS THERE FOR THE TAKING.

Many people spend their lives searching for happiness. In the end, some are fortunate enough to realize that it isn't about having more or doing more or being more. It is about how we view what is already ours.

Look around you today and appreciate the riches God has placed in your life. Even if your circumstances are troubling and your prospects slim, you can always revel in the vibrant colors of the morning sunrise or the amazing tenacity of a dandelion fighting to conquer its place in the grass. When you begin to see and appreciate the richness around you, you will almost certainly find that you have a great deal more to be happy about than you once imagined.

Be content with such things as you have.

HEBREWS 13:5 NKJV